ELIJAH
& THE PROPHETS OF BAAL

ILLUSTRATED BY LAURENT LALO

THE COUNTRY OF ISRAEL WAS IN THE GRIP OF A TERRIBLE DROUGHT. IT WAS JUST AS ELIJAH, THE MAN OF GOD, HAD PREDICTED. NOT A DROP OF RAIN HAD FALLEN FOR THREE YEARS.

THE DISASTER WAS GOD'S PUNISHMENT FOR ISRAEL'S KING AHAB AND HIS QUEEN JEZEBEL WHO HAD LED THEM INTO THE WORSHIP OF PAGAN IDOLS.

ELIJAH TOLD THE KING TO ORDER ALL THE PEOPLE OF ISRAEL TO MEET HIM AT MOUNT CARMEL. HE WAS TO BRING THE 450 PROPHETS OF BAAL WITH HIM.

WHEN THE DAY CAME, ELIJAH AND THE PAGAN PROPHETS FACED EACH AND OTHER, SURROUNDED BY A GREAT CROWD OF PEOPLE.

ELIJAH ISSUED HIS CHALLENGE TO THE VAST CROWD...

HOW MUCH LONGER WILL IT TAKE YOU TO MAKE UP YOUR MINDS? IF THE LORD IS GOD, WORSHIP HIM; BUT IF BAAL IS GOD, WORSHIP HIM!

A HEAVY SILENCE FOLLOWED.

AS EVENING APPROACHED, ELIJAH CALLED THE CROWDS AROUND HIM...

THEY WAITED EXPECTANTLY... WOULD ELIJAH'S GOD DO SOMETHING?

BEFORE THEIR EYES, ELIJAH REBUILT GOD'S ALTAR, USING TWELVE GREAT STONES. THEN HE LAID WOOD ON TOP, CUT THE BULL IN PIECES, AND LAID IT ON THE WOOD.

TO MAKE THINGS HARDER, HE HAD 12 LARGE JARS OF WATER POURED ALL OVER THE OFFERING.

NOW, ELIJAH TURNED HIS ATTENTION TO THE
DROUGHT. ON THE SLOPES OF MOUNT CARMEL HE
KNELT AND PRAYED THAT GOD WOULD SEND RAIN
TO THE PARCHED COUNTRY. HE SENT HIS SERVANT
TO LOOK OUT TO SEA...

SIX TIMES THE SERVANT CAME BACK.
HE COULD SEE NOTHING. THE SEVENTH TIME,
THERE WAS A CLOUD, NO BIGGER THAN A
MAN'S FIST.

ELIJAH SENT HIS SERVANT
STRAIGHT TO KING AHAB, TO
ANNOUNCE THE COMING RAIN.

ELIJAH'S TROUBLES WERE NOT YET OVER. AFTER THE END OF
THE DROUGHT, QUEEN JEZEBEL VOWED TO KILL HIM.
ELIJAH FLED INTO THE DESERT, AND IT WAS THERE, WHILE HE
WAS ALONE AND AFRAID, THAT GOD APPEARED TO HIM AND
GAVE HIM NEW COURAGE. ELIJAH SPOKE OUT BOLDLY FOR GOD TO
THE END OF HIS LIFE.
THE STORY OF ELIJAH CAN BE FOUND IN THE BIBLE, IN
1 KINGS CHAPTER 17 TO 2 KINGS CHAPTER 2.

HODDER AND STOUGHTON EDITORIAL OFFICE 47 BEDFORD SQ
LONDON WC1B 3DP